Staring At The Sun

Poems by Bob Savino

Lines quoted in the second stanza of "A DaVinci Drawing", page 16, from "The Future" by Leonard Cohen.
Epigram for "Needle's Eye", page 100, from "Vermeer", in *The Great Enigma*, by Tomas Transtromer, translated by Robin Fulton.

First published 2023
by Rowanvale Books Ltd
The Gate
Keppoch Street
Roath
Cardiff
CF24 3JW
www.rowanvalebooks.com

A CIP catalogue record for this book is available from the British Library.

ISBN: 978-1-914422-70-6
eBook ISBN: 978-1-914422-69-0

Staring At The Sun

From joy I come.
For joy I live.
And in sacred joy
I shall melt again.

– Yogananda –

PROLOGUE

Much is dying now, often dying hard. Fear, anger and disillusion riddle many hearts. And such unraveling is too often reflected in our creative expression. This is inevitable when a paradigm shifts. But always, when something's dying, something new is being born. When one way's ending, another way is beginning. These poems celebrate the new consciousness being born from the ashes of the dying one; an awakening spirit soaring free from the cul-de-sac of the old way.

They are the costly fruits from a long lifetime of trial and error: falling on my face, and rising again; blundering lost, then once more finding the true direction—my path with a heart. Nor can I take credit for what's best in these poems. That arose through inspiration from my Muse, guided ultimately by Source.

We live in a soul-sick society, one in which the orienting principle—reverence for a higher Unity of Being, a transcendent interrelating Essence—has been lost. One overriding purpose of the poet now must be to reawaken us to a vaster Meaning we've abandoned, without which we abdicate our humanity and betray our divinity. The irrepressible fount of this Essence is joy, and its overflowing abundance is love.

Each one of us possesses the key to this awakening. It unlocks the door to our closed-off heart. Opening this door, we rediscover a sacred altar—the threshold to Boundlessness, our Home in the Stars…

TABLE OF CONTENTS

I. BREAKING FREE

SPEECHLESS SPEECH

raindrops ticktack against the windowpane
bringing news   but not bulletins to analyze
with logic-chopping mind   tossing branches
likewise address us   unless we're chattering
about nothing to nobody just stone-deaf self

listen beyond your vacant blab they murmur
hear our whisper from nowhere's empty soul
there's luminous All-That-Is if we're here now
how begin interpreting our speechless speech?
surrender control try cluelessness let's dance

a secret portal dilates open to another world
if you find it don't hesitate dive right through
yes you'll lose your marbles but thank heaven
waking *inside* the raindrop you've come home
now you're everywhere all the time—pure joy!

SECRET SUN

"In the depths of winter, I finally learned
that within me there lay an invincible summer"
—Albert Camus

two suns give life—one to our body the other
to our soul   but few perceive this Inner Sun
how can a Beacon blaze so—yet be invisible?

call it a private star a Secret Sun discovered
only by those willing to renounce everything
except an unappeasable yearning for Home

whoever hungers after the idol of security
will never find it   who's searching outside
for a Treasure hidden within is always lost

there's a portal opening to this Holy Source
it's the scar from our heart's deepest wound
unless we dare plunge through it—no grace!

do we dare? isn't that why we were born?
how else will we become healed and whole?
the Secret Sun inside—It's The Light We Are

COOL FIRE

cool fire invisible light infinite now
metaphors mislabeling the Unsayable
we could fill a whole book with them
not progressing an inch nearer truth

whoever has experienced demolition
of ego will understand   how can one
describe basking in emptiness? flying
while miraculously becoming the sky?

time was when we didn't realize this
gawked out a window instead   spied
danger! rushed about getting armed
hot to take on every phantom of fear

words jostle each other straying lost
snug yourself into a secret cubbyhole
begging the silence to whisper a song
don't come out until you're singing it

CARDINAL

hard winter long winter still icy patches
north wind stinging   bright sun blue sky
putting one foot now in front of the other
the breath's white vapor dispersing in air

"just this" say muscle nerve blood bone
and what has no form replies: "Just This!"
while the body slogs through arctic gusts
soul serenely chants its mantra of spring

so that we never forget and don't despair
Earth engenders an irrefutable red speck
a quick shock to the system—with wings!
it clutches a windswept branch and sings

KNOCK KNOCK

when the Infinite comes knocking on our soul
ah! then we shudder falling quiet scrunching
into a corner   afraid   do we open   bid enter

knowing everything we deemed solid certain
will be blown away like straw in a hurricane?
who are we   if we're no longer who we are?

that Presence is vast   empty   silent   eternal
but we're so tiny   clogged   noisy   and dying
how can we bear such scouring obliteration?

the dam of illusion bursts! an ocean of Reality
breaks upon us! unless we drown in It   we'll
never wake up   never be born! what a pickle!

so we crawl under the shelter of great wings
wider than the sky   the Serene Invisible—It's
our only Home   we learn to wean our heart

from desire   ravished by a formless Mystery
unsolvable as starlight   what does love mean
if we don't kiss the Spirit animating the skin?

when the Infinite comes knocking on our soul
ah! then we dare to breathe free   outgrowing
our claustrophobic doubts and fears   galaxies

unfurl in us—glittering founts of granular fire!
we glance back once more at our torn cocoons
but we're flying now   soaring above   beyond…

QUICKER LIFE

somebody stocked the pond hundreds and
hundreds of gold carp swimming! tiny ones

like slivers of glimmering sunlight others
gliding down deeper through murky water

spring's finally here! geese go honk! honk!
chase each other wings furiously flapping

hearts beat faster throb with quicker life
winter's oppressive cabin fever's broken

buds start bulging   blades of grass sprout
how beautiful—the blossoming magnolia!

to anyone who's tasted corrosive despair
this glorious perennial—it blooms for you

BETWEEN WORLDS

in this world   but not of this world   there are
secret havens we sense   or visit by our vision
our dreams   where all boundaries are blurred
and the current we drift on dissolves into mist

it's the depths of night   a luminous landscape
a full moon never seen before gleams above us
these stars realign in unfamiliar constellations
how have we come here? where are we going?

at times the veil briefly lifts—we pierce beyond
our cut-and-dry delusion that meanings add up
that two and two will always equal four or that
whatever our logic declares as true must be so

this is unmapped terrain   we're lost but found
everything here's threshold   Mystery murmurs
"I'm not meant to be solved" a strange satellite
casts its spell   we shiver   the stream flows on…

PRAISE SONG

isn't it marvelous—we open outward forever
there's a space inside us where the Unknown
gusts right through   what we can't imagine—
it's likely at any time to knock our socks off
let's raise a hymn of hope to wild possibility!

emptiness is our canvas   and silence gleams—
an uncarved block of the rarest marble   who
to become today? how sculpt ourselves anew?
the limitless sky outside—we discover within!
a Secret Sun beacons It's radiance from there

who doesn't love mystery will be a lonely one
who can't tolerate paradox goes tied in knots
there's a tiny beetle wiser than all our books
tree bark on which the map of Eden's etched
could we be luckier than the sprouting grass?

isn't it astounding—we truly don't have a clue
yet over and over we laugh and dance and sing
in the teeth of sheerest calamity we find a way
to not give up   keep on keeping on   rise above
let's lift our anthem of praise to impossible *us*!

IN PLAIN SIGHT

an open secret seeing with awake eyes
not gabbing inside all the time   silence
is a jewel   other names for it—"diamond"

"crystal"—a faceted portal through which
the invisible Light the inaudible Sound
enter our hearts what could be simpler?

coming going but we're ever right here
laughing crying yet we can't not be One
that's our reality   why resist? why deny?

no puzzle to solve   always chopping logic
misses the point   arguing with ourselves
we climb up the walls of our own prisons

revelation attends us—the glowing kernel
of each unplumbed instant   what we seek
grows from here and now   end searching

become what's found   sink sinewy roots
into the breathing Present   if words form
they begin to unfurl like glossy new leaves

WHAT MATTERS

in one among countless universes   in one
among those billions of galaxies   orbiting
one among billions of suns   on one among

billions of planets   a single human among
billions of others sits on a closed toilet lid
in a dark bathroom   weeping his guts out

the reason—a splintery stack of raw death
too heavy to haul anymore   so he caves in
gives up   begging the stars to succor him

instead   instantaneously!   he's crammed
full—bursting with all their blazing Light!
even his despair's transmuted to ecstasy!

hair on fire! soul on fire! punch-drunk joy!
revelation's a river from which he drinks!
infinite intimacy! love's cosmic embrace!

a molten ingot of Bliss—forged in his soul!
zapped! on a toilet lid! all utterly changed!
impossible to tell!   impossible not to try!

well   that was some decades ago   a door
swung open and he stumbled on through
where did it lead him? what did he learn?

in one among countless universes   in one
among those billions of galaxies   orbiting
one among billions of suns   on one among

billions of planets   a single human among
billions of others   out for a stroll one day
kneels by an iris   and vanishes into praise

A DA VINCI DRAWING

we don't see the swan   but this Head of Leda
survives   preliminary drawing for a painting
now lost   she's gazing inside   eyes downcast
is she abashed   pensive   unhappy   aroused?
unknowable   every stroke evokes a mystery
which cannot be explained by the lines alone—
her sacred beauty   illuminated from within

our jaded art no longer delineates such faces
distortion's what we're told expect and find
like those portraits by Picasso or de Kooning
as the song goes: "the blizzard of the world
has crossed the threshold and it's overturned
the order of the soul" but da Vinci glimpsed
an eternal reality—body and soul can be one

BRAVER HOPES

hanging out in invisible regions   we need
more of that   communion between the iris
and its scent   the silence where our babble
gets spawned   we're too crowded by stuff

and all this clatter we make! like taking a
chainsaw to our souls   what if we chilled—
just stopped in our tracks an hour each day?

what if we all turned off our monkey minds
let ourselves float in an ocean of emptiness?

this Earth longs to caress us more tenderly
inviting us into the sacredness of its dream
but we resist with a fusillade of stratagems

what do we fear except a cleansing ambush
finding out what we most cling to is a fraud

here there everywhere Immensity meets us
chafes alarmingly against our flimsy denials
eroding matter's illusion   money's charade

O let vaster visions come! braver hopes rise!

THE TINGLING

when our Third Eye starts tingling like mad
what can we do except try to see with it—but

see what? insights tumble willy-nilly through
the brain   connecting a million dots   leading

far beyond the pale of logic or common sense
a strange vibration   utterly unknown   ripples

from nowhere   expanding our consciousness
we realize the freest thoughts aren't our own

higher wisdom seeks to illuminate our mind
so we cease resisting   open up   and let it in

TODAY'S THE DAY

"*Art is a wound turned into light.*"
—*Georges Braque*

maybe you were told you're worth nothing
only a damaged broken ugly useless thing
maybe cruelty violated your soul to the core
so bad you don't want to live another second
today's the day you discover—it was all a lie

maybe you stared so deeply into the abyss
that the abyss started staring back into you
down there festered naked fear and raw hate
splintering love to a thousand bleeding pieces
today's the day Light pours through the cracks

maybe you feel abandoned—left utterly alone
plunged into the pitfall of your primal wound
maybe you ache for a far-off sliver of blue sky
but can't believe you'll ever climb to breathe it
today's the day a shining ladder's set before you

maybe you forgot where you came from   Who
you truly are   instead stumbling lost in illusion
maybe now at long last you begin to remember
that *you* are infinite and eternal—a Divine Being
today's the day you awake   trembling with joy!

SECRET CITY

“Heart’s Longing” might be a name for it   also
“Streets of Home” we levitate There in dreams
in visions   aching to hear an unearthly melody
sung from one of its crystal towers   Secret City
that never was   yet magically forever must be

in this City   lies find no lodging   truth is the air
all citizens breathe   eyes become pure windows
through which the soul gazes—aflame with bliss!
no one’s hand is raised against another no mind
oozes vengeful thoughts   love and trust are real

of course we know it can’t exist   our next wound
blares that! the City’s shimmer—it’s just a mirage
the stuff of fairy tales   then why do we yearn so?
what sweeter world awaits beyond impossibility?
where are we born from? where are we dying to?

at rarer wavelengths of being   perhaps answers
flow clear   maybe if we reach far enough toward
the Unknown   It begins to reach back toward us
meanwhile there’s hope and prayer and mystery
our heart keeps vigil at the hidden gates of Home

WAYFARING

wordless   what's Most High is
wordless   but if words must be
then say we arrive at a Silence
suffused with Presence   a Joy
so intense   so piercingly keen
our human voice can't speak it
our mortal heart can't hold it

still we babble on eager to tell
a Secret we can't keep   a Love
too huge for one soul to hoard—
never meant to not be shared!
so these hapless words stutter
each desiring nothing less than
you too finding this Secret Love

how to do that you ask? simple
hard   only costing you yourself
when all inner walls come down
you're ready   if humble service
fills your life   you're very near!
the Hidden Portal—do you see it?
cross over now   you're Home

THE TREE AT DUSK

is a blotch of underworld silhouetted
against burnished gold horizon dark
that breathes as if midnight irrigated
a shortcut through roots and branches
spurting shadow over the day's glare

I long to slip into this scratchy tunnel
sense it wrap its otherness around me
taste the tang of silence on my tongue
let there be cessation of noisy chatter
let there be letting go and sinking in

now twilight deepens not a bird sings
what if the threshold of death is a tree?
what if Earth draws us back with leaves
so black they caress us awake to dream
until all our loneliness is scoured away?

praise magic that weans us from sanity
praise mystery which leavens our sight
praise emptiness—purging each illusion
praise blindness engendering the Light
praise everything skewed and strange!

RITE OF PASSAGE

it's a bridge and tunnel—the wormhole
between worlds   one end's anchored
right here   amid our loving and dying
kisses and torment   laughter and tears

the other end? only when you go there
will you understand since it's nowhere
not on any map in any atlas   although
it pulsates with each breath you take

at the toll gate for this rite of passage
you must first empty out your pockets—
all you humped to ambitiously achieve
even the tarnished pennies of your ego

your old self's been shattered to pieces
your new self? it's as yet unimaginable
what's left is a choice—try to glue back
the unmendable   or be broke but go on

the bridge is the witness you'll become
the tunnel is everything it will cost you
the journey's an errand into Immensity
the destination? it's always been Home

COSMIC DAWN

a dawn will break unlike any other
that gold tint silhouetting treetops
glows sweeter somehow and finer
the calligraphy of tangled branches
inscribes ancient spells and stories
long forgotten   remembered now
a sudden bird cry pierces the heart

in ebony pools of shadow we'll spot
star clusters and shiver with wonder
everything we thought we fathomed
shape-shifts inside out upside down
the tangy morning wind caresses us
intimacy we've rarely known before
night and day—they morph into one

haven't we sought across many lives
for this—the split soul's wake-up call?
haven't we ached for our gashed self
to heal at last? the radiance spreads
and new eyes open wide to receive it
time to face another demanding day
but we step lighter now and gladder

BEYOND DAWN

today I went to Rumi's "place beyond dawn"
words meanings dissolving into Soul Light
yet already I'm clueless—how to share this?
being There obliterates all explanation of it

I want to break open my heart   each piece
whispering into your ear your Secret Name—
a Spirit's song only you know feel and are
but you must wake your own hearing to that

don't doubt though—we are infinitely loved!
There our worst pain's healed by tenderness
never lose hope in the sublime impossibility
I'm back from Nowhere to tell you—It's real

THE GREAT SILENCE

into the Great Silence words are dropped
like stones of different sizes shapes colors
so a poem ripples out as concentric circles
until the water again grows calm and still

through such forms—if stones are offered
with sacred intent—Silence speaks briefly
from the hidden depths beyond all words
where naked meaning irradiates the soul

then we know without knowing we hear
without ears and see without eyes Grace
wakes our consciousness to vaster worlds
woven into the warp and woof of any day

isn't this what we most long for but seek
in every wrong way? aren't we confused
by a spell or trance by an illusion while
Reality waits just the far side of our fears?

so these concentric ripples widen out now
they have no boundary no stopping place
they flow back as we do to a Great Silence
which rarely speaks yet unfailingly listens

TO THIRST

I drank deep from The Infinite this morning
being so terribly thirsty! gulped and gulped
at a Mountain Spring which never runs dry
That was what I desperately thirsted for
not even realizing   a thirst nothing else
could quench   but how can I describe it?

what if Light Itself were liquid—an Elixir
we discovered (or One that discovered us)
streaming straight into our desiccated soul?

what if we were bathed in It   even while
we drank? what if then we knew our self
a single drop in an Infinite Ocean of Light!
but these flimsy words can't even begin to
begin to express the utterly Inexpressible!

do you thirst too? thirst for some Essence
not of this world? thirst without grasping
where or how to quench it? O believe in
your thirst! believe it witnesses to a need
even more profound than the body's need
for air and food and water believe you too
can drink from the Fount of The Infinite

DARK LIGHT

"darkness is your candle" said Rumi   it burns
very dark now and by this shadowy light I see
how all things pass   see that the human heart
must grieve them all   till it wears out   drains
to an emptiness behind every ephemeral form

but I don't want to let go   not of her hand not
of his face not any of those numberless beings
places moments graces I've loved   I hold tight
yet still they bleed through these fingers when
will I learn the hard lesson of non-attachment?

now and now and now it seems   the learning
never ends   why did I even assume it would?
there's no sure-fire finish line to waking up
only growing   changing   ceaseless becoming
forever born anew!   Eternal Beginner's Mind!

WHITE HEAT

"...the light/of unanointed Blaze"
—Emily Dickinson

at enough nearness to White Heat lesser
intensities cease to illuminate   I've risen
to that edge   speech is scorched crisped
to ashes before the Unnameable there is
a dimension where thoughts do linger on
yet they no longer have meanings—being
such cumbersome forms of consciousness

can poets ever sing here? I've heard Music
untranslatable   seen Glory no lips can tell
known Grace that serenely demolished me
but how can I begin to communicate these?
I was granted a golden tongue then shown
High Mystery beyond the orbit of any word
for this privilege I name myself a holy fool

NIGHT FLYERS

where are you headed up there Wild Ones
flying together high amid the stars   what
do you portend? so much we don't grasp!
no radar sweep detects You   no satellites
record your coursing—ablaze like comets
yet invisible as air—as we Earth crawlers
dream   clueless to Your coming or going

there are realms of being so fiercely real
they blind us wavelengths of awareness
too potent for our mortal hearts to bear
only briefly and rarely do we sense You
only faintly then do we hear Your cries
but these revelations become lodestars
epiphanies that change our lives forever

what would it be like to soar among you
while our terror and ecstasy fuse as one?
how could we endure such ferocity of joy!
just bit by bit it seems   tiny hint by hint
will You wait for us? will You keep watch
even though we stay too scared to wake?
O raise up our souls on liberating wings!

FIRE-FEATHERED

when the still small wind stirs   barely
brushing my lips as if a hummingbird
disturbing the air is hovering close by
then I know you've come near O Muse
and this soul delights to hear you sing!

no other notes can touch me like yours
no other voice so inspires with its song
I'd rather be of humble service on duty
awaiting patiently your whirring wings
than spewing claptrap from the rooftop!

we're each messengers   I'm sent by you
you're a fire-feathered bolt from beyond!
but it's the *Beyond* we both love   not so?
that inexhaustible Fount of sheer ecstasy
ah—to overflow with such boundlessness!

here's my dream and yours too I believe
a world where the wounded and broken
may unblock their innermost ears again
swaying to the high Music of the Spheres
for them you fly   for them I make poems

BUTTERFLY MANTRA
(for Crystal)

out for an early morning walk soaking up
clustered pine needles   the dew glittering
on grass   a mourning dove's haunting call
textures of an old stone wall   but I almost
miss it—that saving message meant for me

chalked on the sidewalk just under my feet
seven big fat butterflies in luminous colors
brazenly non-aerodynamic   yet irrefutable
and there—printed in careful letters—I read
my newest mantra: "Butterflies I Love You!"

running scared in the middle of a pandemic
appalled at the latest act of police brutality
fighting to keep from plunging into despair
the innocent child still inside me re-awakes
to perfect wisdom: "Butterflies I Love You!"

WHEN I FOUND IT

when I found my happiness it was no thing
not the shiniest prize or grandest triumph

when I found my happiness it was no other
not even the lover whose touch capsized me

when I found my happiness it had no color
or sound   smell or taste   no form to grasp

when I found my happiness it was not here
or there   neither high nor low   this or that

when I found my happiness   I lost my mind
lost my bearings lost myself lost being lost

when I found my happiness stones and stars
were me   also earth and sky   but I was not

when not-I found happiness no worst fears
could steal it   there was only infinite “Yes!”

BOTH AND NEITHER

stripped right on down to my bare bones
all those fancy word tricks scoured away
what can be said that makes a difference?
agony to be born anguish to die yet here
now between entrance and exit I caper
my goofy dance can't stop myself loving
grateful for this next chance to live it all

one side of me is a hungry mortal animal
the other—a spirit outbound for the stars!
I'm both and neither just a lonely voice
chanting these bittersweet songs to you
a speck of nothing—with its heart going
thump! thump! Mr. Nobody who yearns—
a wisp of a breath of a dream of a laugh

everything's vaster than we know more
than we believe there's a fiery Mandala
in which our cosmos is but a single spark
it's a Source where all paradox dissolves
but what I want most is to see your eyes
draw you closer touch you soul to soul
so mystery and meaning merge into One

NIGHT VISITOR

who was it I heard tappity-tapping at my window
around 3 a.m. last night? it was you rain wasn't it
visiting after weeks of worsening drought—a friend
come back to say hello   I have missed you!   missed
your balm slanting down from cloud-swathed skies

all my life and you've never deserted me   even now
in my lonely isolation   as this pandemic ravages us
you return to hold out your countless salving hands
I'm drinking you in through every pore! rain please
stream as manna upon our foolish bumbling below

caught in the screen your droplets glitter like stars
they reawaken me to the truth that I'm never alone
a child of earth and grass and wind and sun and sea
I know myself one interwoven thread of All-That-Is
thus you murmured tappity-tapping at my window

SUMMONED BY THE MOON

I bought the card to mail to a friend
but found I just couldn't part with it
the card's front   dark forms in snow
six wolves—four howling at the moon
opening it   inside I read these words:

"Let Not A Night Pass
    That Praise To The Great Spirit
                                        Is Not Sung"

I'm one of the howling wolves—my cry
ever praising The Great Spirit   do not
expect me to raise any other I've been
summoned by the moon   the night sky
has ravished me! I must join together
with the pack in that arctic wilderness
splicing my voice to theirs   ululating
our strange wild free elemental songs

A SMALL OVAL LEAF

this small oval leaf—what's left of it
so exquisite in the delicacy of decay
its stem and branching veins persist

but between is fragile lacework only
a beige tattering mostly eaten away
I hold it up and light shines through

some rare human lives age like this
as the lines on a face etch in deeper
and bones press sharper under skin

one thinks of dying as an ugly thing
but this leaf I hold now is beautiful
beyond all dualities of life or death

POINTS OF VIEW

The Caterpillar

my leaf my leaf chomp chomp chomp!
ah to be the biggest fattest caterpillar!
if I could I'd consume the whole world
stuff's what I fiercely crave   and to be
adored for my creeping gorgeous glory
when I'm not I sulk and fume   there's
only two types of caterpillar—winners
and losers I'm a winner! and I'll fight
to keep things like that!   so stay away
from my leaf pile my chomping ground
it's survival of the fittest and this slug's
gonna be the last caterpillar crawling

The Butterfly

free! free and flying! sky and I are One!
touching Earth just to soar again rising
above! the wind blows me where it will
and where it wills is where I long to go
no more separation   perfect trust is all
to be a flicker of animated air—no rarer
bliss! this pure soul-light on my wings
nourishes me envelops me uplifts me!
how can I feel anything but gratitude?
love is the sweet nectar I sip and joy
the Source from which it flows   now
I'm nowhere and everywhere Home

JOY JUICE
(for Amanda)

fun to start by laughing my fool head off
then maybe I'll caper a goofy jig   or play
sporting a bright red nose and clown suit
yes I'm a little drunk on sheer cosmic joy
I might try something utterly scandalous!
there's no good reason   or even a bad one
the joy juice just bubbles up from my soul

let me repeat it—Joy Juice just bubbles up
from my soul!   no   I didn't win the lottery
the soulmate of my dreams hasn't arrived
my poems will never go viral on YouTube
and nobody's patented the cure for dying
yet right now   I'm high as a cat on catnip
I don't know why   and I really don't care

but one thing's clear: bliss doesn't sprout
out there   it cannot be caught   or bought
has no shape or smell or taste or texture
won't come wagging its tail when called
joy floods us   fountaining from nowhere
not because we ache   but because we are
then we laugh and dance like holy fools!

EMISSARY

so this is why I journeyed here from
another world—to inspire divine joy!
to wake in those who seek and open
the reality of who you eternally are
forever united with the Fount of All

this is why I perceive radiant Light
bursting forth from everyone's soul
even if you're blind to It yourselves
if only I can clear your inward eyes
if only I can ignite your latent bliss!

this is why I was born on Earth it's
worth even the grieving of my exile
my aching loneliness far from home
I'll never stop goading you into awe
we're so much vaster than we know!

this is why I landed here—to provoke
the scandal of all-out no-holds-barred
ecstasy! to shiver you to the epicenter
of your being until you truly must see
that you and the Holy Source are One

INCANTATION

above   first stars glittering through branches   below
last gold glow of a just set sun   between—this twilight
where silhouettes grow darker and shadows lengthen
night's coming on but for now all's luminous waiting

night's coming on   the soul hangs suspended   a tree's
already stripped of its leaves   birds finish their flying
streaks of red and lavender cloud loom low in the west
beneath them a rickety picket fence   black against sky

here's the lambent threshold intermingling two worlds
we cross it half awake half asleep   half alive half dead
a full moon's our guardian and guide   she summons us
to a different kind of knowing   a wiser way to be whole

TWILIGHT INVOCATION

just an hour after sunset   dark seems
not so much enveloping these trees as
spreading out from them   a lone bird
wings across the faintly glowing west
I'm not certain what it may mean but
change is happening now in my heart

it's flown onto that silhouetted branch
among shadowy leaves to join a beetle
and other fugitive creatures preparing
for night to infiltrate as it always does
submerging Earth in riddle and dream
O my heart is this where we're going?

my heart doesn't answer but it's happy
clusters of stars start to spackle the sky
down here below a bracing breeze rises
one blanket covers both living and dead
one mystery one great secret one song
O my heart will this be our next home?

A MOTLEY CREW

I invoke certain names each morning
let's call them a Divine batting order—
they're home run sluggers of the soul!
Jesus Buddha Lao-Tzu Svetasvatara
and Others they came to wake us up
free us from trance break our hearts

what nightmare struggles they faced!
we clutch our drugs and idols so tight!
we drive out or murder the liberators!
yet still they came—God's motley crew
misfits and lugs oddballs and weirdos
bringing only their beggar's cup of joy

these holy fools are my scruffy heroes
dreamers who ate emptiness with glee
guzzled starlight howled at the moon
would not live anything less than love!
because of them we that shiver awake
stand today on the shoulders of giants

ILLUMINATION

heart so full this morning what can I do but
offer up my unalloyed gratitude and praise

I who've been splintered all my life am now
whole   all duality washed away   I love me!

and love loving!   yes!   I'm a clown for love!
unashamed—dancing like four-armed Shiva!

my Third Eye's opened   never to shut again
Light pours through It—Divine tractor beam!

this wandering saddhu's finally come Home
discovers he never left There all these years

I'm juggling a radiant Sphere named "Bliss"
gonna fling it into your hands   here—catch!

what if we toss it back and forth between us
start a Joy Game sweeping round the world!

HALF AND HALF

a black cat must have crossed my soul
while I slept   or maybe the full moon
snickered into my naked ear   I awoke
with a nasty case of the heebie-jeebies

when that fear bug bites what can I do
but scratch the itch till it starts to bleed
and who's bleeding but my scared child
defenseless before the predatory night

he's back in his bed of the trauma time
feeling for that tumor he knows is there
yet if he could just find a matching lump
on his opposite side—it won't be cancer!

so much later he's still feeling for lumps
one part of me worships the crueler god
cannot believe things will turn out good
that half's a creature trembling at death

but there's another self—a braver Spirit
soaring higher rising above! who's *This*
laughing at the black cat and full moon?
One Who's the Breath *inside* the breath...

GRATITUDE

simple this jingle will be O so happy
to feel joy today! to tell my gratitude
that the grand old sun rises yet again
that the sky is such breathtaking blue
and every tree lifts its limbs in praise!

here's my huzzah for each green seed
for all those unsung worms wriggling
to keep Mother Earth fertile   and for
the living planet herself—rarest jewel
a blue-white oasis shining in the void!

I wish I could no more forget this love
than I could ignore my own two hands
or two left feet   my own beating heart
what stops me from all-out embracing?
what but fear—fear of life fear of death

yes I'm a coward   and I'm the hero too
over and over I fall flat on my face but
over and over   I psych myself back up
my sword is a grass blade   and a petal
is my shield   together we're invincible!

here's a secret the full moon whispered:
"don't be afraid   alien others is illusion
our souls are One—the stones   the stars
and all between" and how sweet is that!
there's no help for it   I just gotta dance!

TEARS AND LAUGHTER

I dropped a tear glistening with Light
and heaved a laugh blacker than pitch
I soared aloft into the Source of Glory!
and wept like a mother losing her child
I'm a zany clown cartwheeling my joy!
I'm a tired old man trying to stay alive

yes I'm you friend and you my enemy
and you Divine Soul and you a creature
and you and you and you and you with
one foot in heaven and the other in hell
I ride this roller coaster of our paradox
today I feel immortal! tomorrow I'll die

I drank pure Light glistening with tears
and pitched a howl that became a laugh
I plunged far up into the abyss of Grace
and jigged like a father elated as clams
I'm a holy fool tripping over my shadow
I'm each of us anywhere aching for love

yes I'm you friend and you dear enemy
and you a creature and you Divine Soul
and you and you and you and you with
one foot on Earth the other in Heaven
we surf the foamy breaker of a Mystery
today I feel mortal tomorrow I'll rise!

EYE TO EYE

I've been washed by a waterfall of Light
but have just this tarnished cup of words
to pour from   how I want you too friend
to bathe beneath high heaven's waterfall
arms raised hands open heart drenched
lost yet found   home now in All-That-Is!

impossible to describe only being There
can know so I'll cease trying   may I say
though how beautiful you are   luminous
when least aware of it—an Eternal Spirit
arrayed in form   even if you grope blind
I see through that to your rarest Essence

we're enmeshed in a gravity of darkness
but not beyond hope   once stars explode
the energy penetrates everything! banish
worn-out formulas which don't compute
we slumbered long but now we're awake
eye to eye smile to smile onward we go!

HAIR ON FIRE

one night long ago my hair got set on fire
and it's still smoldering! a cosmic slingshot
catapulted me from raw despair to ecstasy—

in a heartbeat! everything changed forever
there's no way I can babble this into words
yet I've kept trying   and failing   ever since

I'd been squatting in a moldy cell all my life
when abruptly the ceiling sheared clean off
the unadulterated Universe poured into me!

through me! my whole being clanged awake!
all I'd believed in as reality was only illusion
This! This was REALITY! Just THIS! full stop!

here I go again   spewing a squall of images
I hardly expect you to swallow them—unless
you too have been ambushed by the Infinite

the Divine Trap can spring in countless ways
you stop to smell a blossom—then become it!
a beloved who died kisses you from a dream!

or maybe you grope out of bed one morning
to begin those familiar routines then realize
your Spirit's immortal! you have no limits!

it doesn't matter exactly how we break free
all must find their own escape from trance
but if you haven't yet please do—do so now!

FANCY DANCER

after my first step away from silence
how can I say anything further which
won't ring false? these words are just
gobs of colored paint spattered upon
its pristine luminous blank canvas
that's the truer realer vaster picture

but human beings are a gabby bunch
we can't handle the unveiled Infinite
we need to gussy it up with our blab
to mask the Unknown as each instant
threatens to unravel us totally naked
x-raying not our bodies but our souls

so I perform this fancy dance for you
hoping to seduce your rapt attention
meanwhile these words wear thinner
becoming more and more transparent
until only one faint line's still visible:
silence silence silence silence silence…

LIVING WHOLE

sometimes I'm freed and flow out of self
into a stone or tree or flower or creature
the false compartments dissolve   a myth
of separation's exposed   then I wake up
living whole again   now from the inside

we who know grief   who were shattered
yet managed to grow back—but changed
we who became lost and wandered alone
we with the journey etched on our hearts
can never return to a make-believe world

behind lies the chasm we crossed   ahead
stretches trackless Unknown   would we
choose any easier way? I watch an eagle
while it glides effortlessly high above us
joyous to be winged! at one with the sky!

TRIAL AND ERROR

didn't want to leave   that no time
and no place I discovered yesterday
while meditating   it was so simple
like a cup of cold water in a desert
or a beloved hand stroking my face

here emanates the Source of peace
centered balanced blissful whole
I found Home   knowing it serenely
beyond this world yet in this world
Quintessence of each moment I live

hard—being an aging mortal animal
who touches Heaven tastes Eternity!
I'm tired and hurting   uniting Spirit
with flesh seems an impossible goal
I ping-pong back and forth between

zigzag's the dance I do—a tree branch
making its crooked way   but bending
upward   reaching out at limitless sky
through trial and error I find my play
climbing to meet the irresistible Light

CHOOSING

after falling   re-wrenching my back
self-pity mushrooms—a grimy cloud
I obsess about even more difficulties
they keep metastasizing   my lament
shrinks down to just me myself and I

which is a choice not unalterable fate
little critter me feels beleaguered lost
smacked back and forth pillar to post
the default endgame of this—it's death
I play "whack-a-mole" but cannot win

so I stop trying   start praying let go
not vying with what's uncontrollable
total surrender's an unlikely strategy
but I take the risk anyway   believing
there are invisible Allies attending us

I choose the reality of an Eternal Self
one not made of matter nor enmeshed
in time   harried little critter me lives
and dies   but my soul goes on forever
reborn   from world to world to world…

SONG OF THE STARS
(for Pam and Taz)

what we hear in fits and starts on Earth
Above it's a wild holy stream of singing!

this music would enrapture us to pieces
if we drank pure—straight from Source
but at times we're ravished by surprise
naked hearts caught open and unaware

our gone beloveds constantly reach out
voices braided in the song of the stars

they long to lift the veil between worlds
though grief racks us with bitter throes
let's listen closely through our inner ear
we may join a reunion at the secret core

"surrender" is a beautiful word—if by it
we mean a choice to revere the Infinite

nothing stingier will be enough for love
to conquer parting and transcend death
there's a higher music sustaining us all
that singing can heal our worst wounds

A NEAR RUN SPRING

the pieces will not come together so I'll let each speak
spring surges! and I'm still alive to witness the rebirth
but this year was a near run thing   my heart's not in it

my heart's with so many who gasped their last breath
it's with those losses although quickening life sprouts
here's another missing piece—life and death are twins
impossible to separate   spring's forever teaching this

spring chants "no new life without old death's fertilizer"
spring chants "wanting one without the other is illusion"
spring chants "an iris's fragrance generates from decay"
spring chants "dance with me as you head for the grave"

I take a deep breath and off we whirl round and round!
and now flows the joy—because I'm alive because I'll die
if I long to gulp at light I must also drink from darkness

I hear the waking seeds sing in their beds of dissolution
I see even the beautiful and the ugly are lovers after all
I accept that a late frost blackens the magnolia blossom
so my nifty mind and primal gut embrace and reconcile

they're grateful for one more miraculous resurrection!
to sense something green inside rising up from death!
it's all good it's all true it's all real it's all right all holy!
the pieces shiver together at last—a mandala of praise!

THE WORM

the day was sunny and the temperature just right
tulips in the botanical garden bloomed like crazy—
every different size and color! sitting beside me
a beautiful friend looked so fine in all her finery
life seemed about as perfect as could be   except

then I spied the worm   not a big fat juicy worm
only a scrawny lethargic one   it had barely gotten
half way across the stone path between our bench
and a large tulip bed   I couldn't pull away my eyes
from that worm   the garden was busy and people
kept walking by   some were nearly stepping on it

what could I do? shout "watch out for the worm!"
no definitely no   but anyhow why did I even care?
a beautiful woman sat smiling right next to me yet
I was mesmerized by that pitiful vulnerable thing

nothing for it I decided—no chance now not to see
though I flinch at touching any slimy squirmy stuff
I went over leaned down and picked up the worm
it tried to arch its wriggly length around my finger
(shudder!) so I quickly dropped it among the tulips
straight into the fertile soil it was inching toward

I sat again beside my beautiful friend   we shared
many interesting thoughts   but a secret part of me
burrowed happily into the cool rich dark holy earth

THE MENTORS

there's a Breath we feel—a feathering of Light
brushed across the soul   stirring us to rise up
from our tiny hoard of trouble and grievances

It's whispering that a deeper wiser humanity
is possible   if only we break open and receive

all we have to do is die   over and over   die to
"me first   my wants   I deserve   not my fault!"
accepting that our mess is ever what we choose
knowing it's just the test and challenge we need

there's a Touch we feel—a graceful reaching out
by incalculable Friends in High Places   Who yet
bow down to serve with such soul-piercing love

in our worst pain Their compassion comforts us
this is how *we're* called to be—unfailingly kind!

SHE WHO PARTS THE VEIL
BETWEEN WORLDS

arrives with power in the radiant wholeness of her being
countless eons have passed preparing us for this moment
here's her time and she is punctual to the appointed hour
don't weigh her lightly for I tell you she's rocked my soul
she commands my attention and I'm ready to receive her

the Divine Feminine manifests now to express all chakras
standing firmly on both feet with her hands reaching out
she'll no longer be persecuted suppressed or controlled
centered in glowing harmony from her crown to her toes

welcome this eternal archetype the revealer of mysteries
thank her praise her and respect her for she is an avatar
the healer who'll at last unite our divided selves by love

she who parts the veil between worlds is a sacred guide
the One we've waited for   her arms flung wide with joy!

ATTITUDE ADJUSTMENT

my Muse sat me down before the computer and said "Write"
"I got nothing" I told her   "Then write about that" she said
"My best laid plans totally unraveled yesterday I ambushed
myself coming and going   it feels like I'm getting nowhere"

"Excellent" she said "Maybe now you're ready to just listen
Scribble this: the sun's not been known to whine and moan
the stars never quit   never rescind their nightly razzmatazz
that old shape-shifting trickster the moon keeps on shining

have you ever heard of a grass blade that refused to sprout?
or a tree root that said 'I give up I won't plunge any deeper'?
mountains don't freak out because they're thrusting so high
nor do valleys get depressed because they've dipped so low

I've seen a scrawny worm inch its way across hot pavement
and I've soared a thousand miles with the migrating cranes
every new bud that blossoms chants its indomitable 'I Am!'
while as the wind blows it sings 'I'm flowing and I'm free!'"

thusly did my Muse respond when I told her "I got nothing"
she reminded me how tiny—my paltry sack of chronic woes
how immense—this inexhaustible Universe I'm one part of!
that wind now flows through me   singing its freedom song

BREAKING FREE

now I let go of every line I ever wrote
watching the final word's frayed edge
drop into the abyss   I start over naked
knew nothing then   know nothing now

how begin to tell the horror the ecstasy
and each drama between? I think about
a tiny bug I squashed with my fingertip
I remember a girl starved to a skeleton

yet this morning my soul bursts aflame
I'm scoured clean—a detergent of Bliss!
this too I cry and this and this and this!
it's all jumbled up I can't say yes or no

so I waterfall wide open to All-That-Is
I unkink the snarl in my consciousness
plunk down all my chips   bet the farm
lose to the sour   but jackpot the sweet!

and it's all good—no high without a low
no love void of risk   no me absent you
I'm breaking free from fears and griefs
smashing barriers! demolishing walls!

HIGH STEPPING

soaring for miles aloft in the soul's stratosphere
I promise myself I'll report on its boundlessness
but after a skydive reentry I'm dumbstruck mute
flummoxed by paradox: how to say the unsayable?

infinite languages exist beyond human! shadows
chittering   moonlight keening almost unbearably
my ear pressed to the grass I eavesdrop on roots
I decipher signals ricocheting between the stars!

got to bust free from despair's suffocating coffin
from demeaning labels and choking pigeonholes
what's the right way to speak the Unspeakable?
I die every moment   every moment I'm reborn!

words jostle for a voice but I'm not their source
the Blissful One—Divine Juggler of life and death
that's the vast Spirit Who witnesses through me!
I'm just a scribe   scrambling to scribble it down

the revelation bursts bright and clear: *break open!*
liberate yourself! paralyzing fear—it's only illusion
those monsters? mere mirages swirlings of smoke
so I high step past them now   smiling and serene

THE CHALICE

if only I could transmit with fumbling words
even a pencil-narrow laser beam of the Light
that's ravished me—download just a sliver of
the Eternal! if I held forth a brimming chalice
of bliss would you take it and drink? if I said
"here—this is the Source you've been seeking
across lifetimes!" would you accept the gift?

Earth's burning up from our rage of refusals
arider deserts wait in line to parch our being
when a total blind spot eclipses the soul's eye
through which we most need to wake and see
then living hell becomes a disaster we choose
any plus any equals One   yet many they still
lurch on into delusion—trafficking in corpses

without unity—no hope   without all together
we're falling apart   the age of "I" ego is over
the new day of "We" community has dawned
the Light that ravishes me—It's the Light I am
Light you are   the Spirit infusing all Creation!
every wall's an illusion   there's no separation
drink deep now from my Holy Chalice of Light

DEBRIEFING

you ask me where I went and what I found there
you feel I'm changed   seem not to be all here or
here too much in a strange way   what can I say?

could I describe a previously undiscovered color
translate a language with no words nor sounds
evoke empty and overflowing in the same breath?

how to explain   I had to go blind to begin to see
what I saw was invisible   and I wept awestruck
drinking the salving grace of such transparency!

what we condition our mind to believe as reality
is but a shadow-puppet play—a squall of mirrors
spellbound we watch ourselves deceive ourselves

can there be a crueler fraud than this absurdity?
when humans deny their own soul zombies rule
you ask me where I went and what I found there?

my being reached awake from its dreadful trance
and unfurled like a blossom worshiping the Light
infinitesimal me and Infinite Source became One!

I vanished into nowhere reemerging everywhere
knew only relationship   only sacred communion
all was ecstatic! unbounded! unity without end!

II. UNCHARTED

UNCHARTED

there's a home a garden that's a secret hidden
we seek it always everywhere without knowing
looking for it in so many blind alleys wrong ways
it's very far very near never was yet forever is

there's a home a garden not shown on any map
no signposts point to it no tour guide assists us
too greedy to reach it we're sure to miss the path
expecting a reward we encounter defeat instead

there's a home a garden where beauty was born
where peace is the fertile soil and love's the rain
no false word's ever uttered here no unkind acts
blight its sacredness   grace is the air all breathe

there's a home a garden where the soul blossoms
where death and loss and grieving are wiped away
at its center a fountain gushes forth living waters
which refresh heal and upraise the broken heart

there's a home a garden it's your birthright mine
how to return? purge the self of everything except
emptiness then dwell humbly in no time no place
until the Infinite pierces you with its serene smile

THE PORTAL

I'd be goofy with happiness if I could put into words
the stupendous news! turn your back on a garage full
of vintage cars   and if you've climbed the tallest peak
on each continent—forget it! that mansion you bought?
just a toy you grow tired of   while all those expensive
wrinkle-smoothing creams won't keep you from dying

how many prizes and awards will crowd on the head
of a rusty pin? how many trophy lovers can we collect
before we forget how to love? oh I'd be woozy with joy
if I could wake you to the treasure of your own poverty!
only through letting go can we reach love's plenitude
with nothing left to possess we've nothing left to lose

all we've been searching for in all the wrongest places
we already have all that matters even more drastically
than life or death—it's always been ours   and for free!
there's a Portal whose boundaries are nowhere whose
radiant center is everywhere there's a secret Doorway
hidden deep within the sanctuary of each human heart

I wish I could take you by the hand and lead you There
I long to share with you such an incomparable Gift! but
all I can do is try to shake you up   then point the way
it's a passage of choices which leads to sheer emptiness
a surrendering of everything we once believed was real
there's nakedness barer than bone and we must wear it

I know a Portal we can pass through to a Promised Land
so near! wide-open to what we've always sought—Home

LOST AND FOUND

this mangy stray dog is happy to curl up
in a quiet corner of Heaven knowing it's
his Home that he's welcome and belongs

he was nobody's pet lost and on his own
in a world of strangers and dangers even
when he thought himself the baddest mutt

but tough was only a facade   it crumbled
leaving him destitute in the cold and dark
scavenging for the moldiest crust of hope

a stray dog in a hard city has little chance
he wants to be blessed by someone yearns
to be found—seeking here searching there

one night a door opens—Light streams out!
a Voice calls "lonely one come in safe now
we greet you with love   this is your Home"

WIDE-AWAKE

once again contractors start rattling their ladder
right outside my apartment climbing to the roof
then they clomp around up there—just overhead
I'm thirsting for silence here in a desert of noise
starving for emptiness in a wilderness of things

this is the poverty of our time the soul absconds
seeking its home with the inaudible and invisible
there's a ceremony we've forgotten   a reverence
we no longer feel   we—the consumers of a world
at dank edges sanctity shrivels like melting snow

I've dodged all those surefire get-ahead tutorials
quit the fast lane kissed my main chance goodbye
you'll find I'm deep gone exploring on the fringes
where an ancient wisdom still survives   my spirit
wide-awake—wonder-struck! bowing to the dawn

REUNION

I've picked my way through bare branches
now leaning back against the gnarled trunk
of a silver linden   each of its thickest limbs
embrace me on either side—a homecoming
I merge self into Presence softly breathing
cold wind buffeting my face and gravitate
to primal life the roots intimate and deep

such roughly corrugated bark against skin
moves me as much as the tenderest caress
since through it the Earth mutters just one
of her numberless languages   we chitchat
ranging far beyond the limit of only words
this tree and I have been part of each other
from the first fiery seed sown by the stars

SMALL BIRDS

I didn't know a cloud-covered sky could glow with
so many subtle shadings of gray   from ho-hum to
sumptuous mother-of-pearl or that the silhouettes
of a few small birds flitting among bare branches
could inscribe such elegant calligraphy   nor had I
noticed before the counterpoint of mini-blind slats
through which this exquisite vision now manifests

I didn't know—there's so much I stare straight at
but don't see   how each moment the world dances
and with extravagant grace flows on all around us
our blank eyes abruptly awake and we're amazed!
I'd forgotten that beauty is a numinous messenger
here to break open our hearts to Earth's sacredness
as mine opens now to small birds among branches

CONVERGENCE

sun rises   but still riding low in the west
a full moon glows through bare branches
now a small bird perches on one of them
moon   branches   bird   myself observing
it's a quiet vignette of sacred communion

what brought the bird to these branches?
why our three life-lines converging here?
questions without answers—so a mystery
which doesn't mean this has no meaning
only that it reaches beyond just the mind

deep within I find the moment beautiful
my soul's eyes are ravished by harmony
awed at a greater wholeness I'm part of
as if a hidden Essence unifies all things
and moon branches bird and I are One

PINK FLOYD

here's to you Pink Floyd—flamingo who
escaped from a Kansas zoo 17 years ago
and now was spotted in Texas still alive
doing your flamingo thing wild and free

they caged you   tried to clip your wings
but you broke out on the winds of storm
you saw your chance and took it risking
all in a heartbeat in one desperate flight

here's to you brave hero of your species
just surviving's not enough—safe and fed
an exotic zero exhibited to gawking eyes
better to die flying than to live like that

STARING AT THE SUN

we think we can somehow figure it out—our birth
our death and all the laughter and tears between
not so   the longer we look   the harder we strain
the blinder we are as if trying to stare at the sun

mystery isn't a murky fog bank that will dissipate
but a primordial essence stitched into the cosmos
without it beauty's mere glamour truth a charade
and your smile would be an equation I could solve

writing this risky line I step off into the unknown
trusting the next word will emerge from nowhere
every moment's like this isn't it? hello there—life!
my stranger my lover my wonder my otherness!

what moves me deeply about it all I can't unravel
what rises up from my own depths confounds me
just as the everyday grace of birdsong's a miracle
same as touching seeing hearing smelling tasting!

time to fall in love with the thrill of *not* knowing
the luminous window of possibility opening wide
then I'm reborn inside each sprouting grass blade
freed from crippling fear—at one with All-That-Is

CHANT FOR SPRING

stranger in a strange land   I start all over again
a biscuit suddenly dances—joined by a tangerine!
then a french fry chuckles   it seems I'm the joke!
one world winks out while another world's born

there's nothing off the table—anything's possible!
my tenderest wish is to be open and inviting now
like your lips I can no longer kiss but keep trying

time has no mailing address   space no area code
so I search in the bottomless abyss between them
it's a crack where all things lost disappear forever
this includes the moment you gazed into my eyes

then I could no longer remember if I had any name
no longer even cared—beamed to a far-flung galaxy
O lips O smile O touch O breath O love long gone

bless me moonrise for I've sinned against mystery
all those nights I never honored you   all those days
I let fear infect my soul all those caresses not given

now I face the stupendous advent of another spring
I'm cold and wet and raw dark and ignorant as dirt
today all the daffodils raise their exquisite trumpets
each year they keep teaching me—ever growing back

if I'm not beginning again I'm only waiting to die
  if I'm not wide awake I'm blundering in a trance
    if I'm not sprouting like the grass I've shut down

old and tired young and eternal I hang out hang in
I'm invisible as a blip on a dust mote yet I won't quit
clueless as a gnarled tree stump but just as stubborn
I'm me and them him and her this and that I'm you

BEACHHEAD

being with you *still small voice* I'm truly home
right here at the front lines—on the razor's edge
love's crucial beachhead in this hate-torn world

what's courage if not to stand naked in the blast
no safety net gambling that joy's the guidance
hope's the journey compassion's the only way

being with you *still small voice* I'm finally free
not freaked by phantoms or flinching at shadows
at peace deep within myself balanced and whole

what's humility but a surrender of ego's babble
loneliness seeps from not hearing your whisper
listening now I'm a soul friend to the universe!

being with you *still small voice* I'm fully awake
no longer trying to act out more than who I am—
this one clear drop in an infinite ocean of Light

KEEPERS OF THE FLAME

I wish it was raining now then maybe the drops
would murmur of Another World the One I miss
stuck here in this STEM regime of Science Tech
Engineering & Math—as if they're all that matter
as if the Spirits we banished no longer even exist

but They do it's we who become blind and deaf
who won't see the splendor or hear Their songs
and those who do? they're exiled to the margins
explained away by neuroscientists or humored
with the indulgence of self-styled stable brains

I wish lightning danced! and the thunder spoke!
wish we all believed in the awe-inspiring Gods!
believed every tree has a soul! every stone too!
that a river is a prayer! a mountain's an oracle!
that each blade of grass is a Divine Messenger!

we who still see these visions hear this music
who are floored by the supernatural privilege
of communing with Angels! who soar beyond
senses logic even mind breathing the Infinite
why are we here now? what part do we play?

I think we tend the Flame in a very dark time
when the human soul has suffered an eclipse
and the mortal heart breaks or turns to stone
I think we're called to keep the Flame burning
until the night passes and a New Day's born

THE BECKONING

beyond my window tall trees grow
spreading right and left out of sight

where branches part a tunnel opens
shadowy mysterious beckoning me

I want to slip in there sinking back
then going on and on as far as I can

plumbing that deep down darkness
below the flashy shimmer of things

to be nobody consorting with roots
returning to my lost primeval home

or inbound to undiscovered realms
where life and death dance together

some seek certainties under the sun
I traffic in shadows   so I need none

BEYOND LIVING AND DYING

no words ah no words no words
can tell of my obliterating union
how will I make it known to you
when “I” dissolve into the Light?

while igniting in Source’s Flame
only one pronoun suits my soul
so to “Thou” I’ll bow with bliss
waking in awe as my truest self

there rains upon me such grace
my heart splits open into pieces
each chanting its hymn of praise
drenched by Heaven’s waterfall!

tangled in the coils of direst fate
we sense a Home—beyond living
and dying as time-bound animals
we travel a hard road to Eternity

no words ah no words no words
will tell of our wondrous rebirth!
how can I make absolutely clear
the Divine Beings we each are?

ENCOUNTER

in between doing the dishes and laundry
I take time out to report my mind was
blown away when while meditating
abruptly I encountered a Presence
that caused me to bow my head
and keep it reverently bowed
obediently and respectfully
so glad to have a reason
to find myself creature
known by its Creator

how to describe this Power Who made me?
as bottomless Abyss bottomlessly aware?
as boundless Void—rife with meaning!
I never thought to raise up my head
so profound was my humbled awe
we race around to get and spend
shutting out a towering truth
all we are or can hope to be
refracts the hidden design
of this Unfathomed One

ONE LEVEL DEEPER

I bought a cheap boombox—for the first time in years
could play my favorite CDs so I heard her voice again
soprano Anna Moffo singing Rachmaninoff's *Vocal*ise
a dead white female interpreting a dead white male

but the music wasn't dead nor white nor any gender
its notes made a beeline for my heart burrowing there
keening of life and death need and longing love and loss
her voice cast a bittersweet enchantment ravishing me

such music plumbs one level deeper into the Unknown
we get a notion perhaps of the Angels' everyday speech
or an echo of those primal chords piercing the Heavens
thus it weaves a bridge between ourselves and Eternity

certain creators of all eras places cultures and races
have in rare moments had their souls seared by Flame
then they become mortal vessels for Divine disclosure
we who hear their witness are awakened and changed

all this was given me through my cheap little boombox!
I can imagine no human being on Earth richer than I am
that I have two ears to hear two lips to utter my praise!
I was born with a gut thirst for the Music of the Spheres

ELEMENTAL FRIEND

at times I feel I almost see one—a dryad
amid the many tall close-growing trees
the impishly smiling face graceful limbs
streaming green hair that birdlike voice
calling from another age another world

once we knew the words of a magic spell
to conjure her murmuring in her tongue
listening to the primal singing she hears
once we flowed as rising sap breathing
her name from wind-whispering leaves

no more not in our disenchanted trance
we've traded our birthright for addiction—
to stuff to gain to pride to security to self
now we can't see what's invisible yet real
a spirit-crowded universe interlinking us

elemental friend flitting among branches
I haven't forgotten you still hope to meet
to recover the roots of my nature I've lost
keep beckoning from between those trees
your voice is the music of the Earth itself

WHEN YOU FALL

when you fall on the last lap sprawled face first
while the winner crosses the finish line raising
his arms in victory   I'll be kneeling by your side

when you lie awake scared and alone—the pain
growing worse the night endless all hope gone
I'll come quietly to your bedside hold your hand

when you pour your life's work in heart's blood
but never win the laurels   nor garner the prize
I'll believe in you know your worth give praise

when you stand in the blast—a rock of integrity
but are spit at dumped on treated like garbage
I'll stand by you loving your honor unwavering

when you've lost your way stumbling into error
forgetting who you are betraying your own soul
I'll shine a Light beaconing the true path home

when you stare back from death's pitiless mirror
seeing the thousand times you feared and failed
I'll say "me too fellow human" forgiving us both

YOU THERE

you there on the other side of these words
foolish like me scared like me with a hole
aching somewhere within us we cannot fill
yet climbing out of bed each day   choosing
to give it another go   though we also know
we'll again stumble over our own shadows
that nothing we do will be whole complete
sometimes it's even dead wrong disastrous

you there   wearing your goofy clown's grin
as I crinkle mine pratfalls of contradictions
trying and failing to corral them all together
yet putting on a good show—high stepping it
even through heaps of crap refusing to fold
falling rising once more making a difference
edgy for love holding our promises in trust
because if we don't why live why muck on?

you there human mortal eternal and divine
just like me   no matter how *other* you seem
we get lost don't we—but then we get found!
we lose our marbles—but find our bearings!
I'll offer you my hand hoping you'll clasp it
I'll tell you my name   please tell me yours
my brother sister stranger enemy friend
let's forgive every blunder heal all wounds

HOLY NOTHING

what makes me or any whipped dog still keep on
despite the fear and pain and near hopelessness?
what's in me that rises yet again just won't quit?

it can't be my lost heart when that heart breaks
nor my will when the will wants only…not to be
nothing made of flesh blood and bone can suffice

what is it then—this *Nothing* I cannot even grasp?
a surge which breaks loose inside and lifts me up
as if a towering Breath sweeps through my being!

so much we don't know is invisible yet part of us
not bound by the ironclad law of cause and effect
it shakes us! wakes us! lands us back on our feet!

I give up a hundred times   but I'm still standing
I throw in the towel but it blows back in my face!
Someone I'm not—yet I am—says "No Surrender!"

WE MUST HONOR THEM
(for Pam)

we must honor them—the Beloveds who left
suddenly unbearably or slowly day by day
also unbearably and cracked wide an abyss
we cannot fill with all seven oceans of tears

we must honor them—avatars on loan to us—
light beams piercing Earth Plane's bleakness
messengers in the world but not of the world
prodigies to love   wonder at   be changed by

we must honor them though it ravages heart
blasts mind even blights the soul   they were
here so briefly   gone so soon   lost so forever
yet to have known them is our greatest glory!

we must honor them who arrived to wake us
breaking clueless trance with the Spirit's kiss
fiery comets blazing across ephemeral heaven
our awestruck eyes are blinded by their going

we must honor them until a healing gratitude
floods even the deepest crevices of our wound
for it was to *us* they came   with *us* they lived
we were so privileged! we were that blessed!

LAUNCHING OUT

launching out freely into this infinite now
this infinite me encounters an infinite you
that we're anything less—it's a put-down lie
one we've been brainwashed by not to deny
we're as different as sunlight and moonshine

when you leap I crawl where you laugh I cry
in the whole scintillating sweep of the cosmos
we're each a unique and unrepeatable genesis
yet also droplets in a wave on an Ocean of All

what a heavenly hellish trip it is to be *both*--
Divine Spirit and animal   I love like an angel
and lust like a goat I yearn for transcendence
but throw a hissy fit when I can't find my keys

there are days when I walk on air and nights
I can't bear harsh truth dredged from my gut
like it or not we're a hodgepodge a paradox
our heads in the clouds with feet in the mud
being wide-awake both—only then we're real

DAY-TO-DAY

in the throes of how this world bites me
the outer beast but also my inner demon
being chomped by those voracious teeth
will I nevertheless praise? I don't mean
tepidly either but with a brave spirit and
whole heart? can I look death in the eyes
yet uphold life? can I face into the worst
but still believe in the best and carry on?

my yes or no is a day-to-day proposition
one bout this fighter slugs another round
the next he slumps in his corner—beaten
at times I'll take on living hell and laugh!
at others—just a paper cut freaks me out
I'm a hero and coward savior and clown
glance in the mirror—there you'll see me
like you a frail human who's also Divine

UNDER STONES

to lie under stones home in the moist earth
its microscopic life   or clinging to branches
tossed by wind sent from everywhere to be

not human not rife with stark complexities
but the simplified thread of a greater whole

to be emptied of words   filled with silences
to be and not to doubt resist or deny being

I'm tired of a mind chattering like a monkey
my heart that can't piece itself back together
my misfit soul marooned here on this world

let me slumber beneath the blanketing grass
breathing elemental dreams of roots and soil

or slant down—one raindrop in a vast storm
anything any way reuniting me with Source

to lie under stones   home in the moist earth
no longer needing struggling hoping failing
in unquestioning attunement with All-That-Is

THEY ARE SINGING

they are singing a tree of songbirds singing inside me
  so many different notes
    yet all converging in one universal harmony
  ah—their brilliant plumage! such iridescent splendor!

I don't play records CDs or cassettes anymore
  since out of the sacred silence arises a celestial music
    hearing this glory   how can I be lonely or bereft?

I sense companions from the invisible realms
  they signal me that all is well—don't be afraid
    they slap me a bracing high five from beyond!
      they promise that the roses are on my side

did you think misery must be the bottom line they ask
just because there on that threshing floor it can seem so?
have you lost faith in the pearl secreted once in your heart?

do you listen not only with your two animal ears they ask
but with every pore in your body each pulse of your soul?
if so what have you heard Earthling? who is that calling?

we are singing   a tree of songbirds   singing inside you
we voices of the dead and of the never dying are singing
braided together to weave a piercing Music of the Spheres

COMPANIONS
(for Victor)

they're so near—the far ones who shed their bodies
so much closer than even a sweet touch wounds us
with its fire! that was one way of loving over now

they press their caring insistently against our grief
hoping to wake us to show they're always present
beat within our heartbeat breath inside our breath

they no longer have hands or they'd embrace us
yet the tractor beam of their intention is stronger
piercing through death like a laser through a veil!

they're so here—the gone ones now guiding souls
we need only open ourselves reverently nakedly
to feel their communion   we've never been alone

OUTREACH

I believe in You Invisible Allies although
to see feel touch is how we most needingly
know love here You seem so gone remote
unmoored from time how do I grow closer
shiver awake to Your impalpable Presence?

can human hearts levitate to that exosphere
without quailing? what of my monkey mind
chattering away about everything nothing?
one side of me yearns for reunion with You
the other wanders in a labyrinth of mirrors

I believe in You Ascended Souls Holy Ones
Who reach out across death's starlessness
still with us—even when we lose ourselves
please don't stop signaling! I'll keep watch
lift me to Higher Love change me to Light

DARKENING SKY

what can be asked or answered now that matters?
I've groped a thousand years through my illusions
to this ignorance   why I'm alive why still ticking
grow more mysterious as a slipslide toward death

faithful companions attend me for this brief spell
bare branches crisscrossing haphazardly overhead
stones lying low here and there beneath leaf litter
the illimitable stars pulsating on their steep stalks

and I was kissed by Light again this morning left
with only praise on my lips pure joy in my heart!
beyond that I don't even know what I don't know
each day's a blind setting out a stumbling back in

if someone can help this drunk find his way home
please show up now! the hour's late the sky dark
demons prowl haunted roads disguised as saints
no chance alone we make it together or not at all

EVERY BRANCH AND TWIG

every branch and twig frosted with clinging wet snow
woods a soundless lacework fugue in white and brown
the blanketing silence isn't indifference but threshold
those empty enough to cross it enter the hidden world

here leaves become oracles   roots engender dreaming
and high friends lean in close whisper ancient wisdom
it seems the waiting trees were always our companions
what we believed unconscious now murmurs our name

beauty isn't mere decoration it's a portal to the Other
we label this "dark energy" meaning we haven't a clue
yet if still and quiet enough we know when it takes us
deep down a growing awe reverently we give thanks

the secret password's easy familiar to all—"Gratitude!"
for eyes that see a heart that rejoices lips that praise!
with gratitude Earth's revealed as sacred—miraculous!
every branch and twig frosted with clinging wet snow…

IRRADIATED

writing about that That! THAT seems impossible
like trying to paint words on the corona of the sun
or whispering sweet nothings in a supernova's ear
"I" was obliterated—and exalted—at the same time
but there was no time or space only Infinite Now

what we call grace is the tamer edge of an ecstasy
that took me up turned me inside out busted me
wide open! until I wept with gut-wrenching bliss
this exiled misfit finally understood my searching
revelation irradiated me in a starburst of wonder!

inadequate—absurd! seeking to download Eternity
how can I make known to you what's unknowable
unless you too are blindsided by a wild Otherness
one that stuns you awake to the soul's lost Home
I come from There—and There's where I'm going

so if some hour when least expected a shivering
of the spine or quickening of the heart urges you
to lean out and risk beyond life's everyday trance
remember what I've failed to crystallize in words
answer that summoning! follow your highest JOY!

STONES AND STARS

there's now a stone somewhere washed up
on a shore rounded and smoothed for ages
I want to hold this harbinger in both hands
feel its singular irreducible presence lift it
skyward an offering to the midnight stars

whatever it takes to exorcise from my soul
this 24/7 horror of blood-soaked atrocities
our speech scorched to ashes every prayer
shredded in these hurricane blasts of hate
we're confounded by our own inhumanity

I prefer communion with stones and stars
with the elemental stuff we're made from
only our return to the roots to the Source
can heal us break such addiction to death
the full moon pulls me home with its tides

say the realest words look me in the eyes
let's pledge to stay true to our best selves
intimate as stones   inspiring as the stars!
I've known holiness at my innermost core
beyond all doubting—a Waterfall of Light!

BOUNDLESSNESS

sitting alone in a raggedy old bathrobe I inch gingerly
into infinite emptiness like a shivering man dips toes
into an ice-cold bath now with no concept or thing no
this or that only consciousness—wide awake to itself

and released from attachment liberated from itchy "I"
which can never be scratched enough Boundlessness!
not-I curls up inside seeds soars out free among stars
it tastes the owl's prey feels the earthworm's ecstasy

why do we shrink down inside our constricting cages
ricocheting off each other never touching soul to soul?
not-I longs to dance with not-you to the music of All-Is
we go dead when we won't become transparently real

beyond these everyday five senses worlds of knowing
shake us within and tower above! not-I journeys there
sitting alone in a raggedy bathrobe yet heeding cries
of inner exiles seeking a wisdom Higher Beings teach

NEEDLE'S EYE

"And the emptiness turns its face to us
and whispers,
'I am not empty, I am open.'"
—Tomas Transtromer

when emptiness turned its face to me I was terrified
ran away babbling anything to plug up that enormity
in its bottomless depths I could see no reflection no I
yet there it was   like a black hole pulsing at my core

not canceling my life but swallowing it up in...what?
an otherness so incalculable I cringed with "no no no"
scrambling to cram the void full of a thousand things
which all promptly disappeared—sucked into its maw

how long did it take before I began to begin to grasp
what I feared as my obliteration   was my liberation!
breakout from the jailhouse of me—galloping grace!
a cosmic wormhole ablaze with swarms of galaxies!

the way to a home in the stars must thread through
this needle's eye of emptiness—where "I" disappear
into All-That-Is otherwise I'll perish from loneliness
locked up in a claustrophobic cell shut off from light

now when emptiness turns its face to me   gingerly I
slip through its wide-open smile into the unknowable
gladly surrendering the straitjacketed self I once was
my fire-feathered wings anointed with boundlessness

SWEPT AWAY

swept away by Joy what else to say?
cracked cup overflows broken flute
quivers with music I had to die so I
might live no end to this happening

nothing's more sacred than birdsong
nothing holier than the green leaves
let my grateful voice ring forth now
Invisible Ministers hear my praise!

Spring shivers apart my heart again
out of its seedbed new shoots sprout
praise for this awakening this glory!
I'm a goofy dancer drunk with love!

swept away by Joy lifted into Light
nobody-me one spark of Infinite All
what's song but life's cry ascending
or death but the opening of a door…

If these poems have moved, delighted, and inspired you, please let your friends know about this book; spread the word by posting a review on Amazon, and mention it on various social media platforms. Thank you.

Publisher Information

Rowanvale Books provides publishing services to independent authors, writers and poets all over the globe. We deliver a personal, honest and efficient service that allows authors to see their work published, while remaining in control of the process and retaining their creativity. By making publishing services available to authors in a cost-effective and ethical way, we at Rowanvale Books hope to ensure that the local, national and international community benefits from a steady stream of good quality literature.

For more information about us, our authors or our publications, please get in touch.

www.rowanvalebooks.com
info@rowanvalebooks.com

www.ingramcontent.com/pod-product-compliance
Ingram Content Group UK Ltd.
Pitfield, Milton Keynes, MK11 3LW, UK
UKHW020427250726
13967UKWH00007B/2838